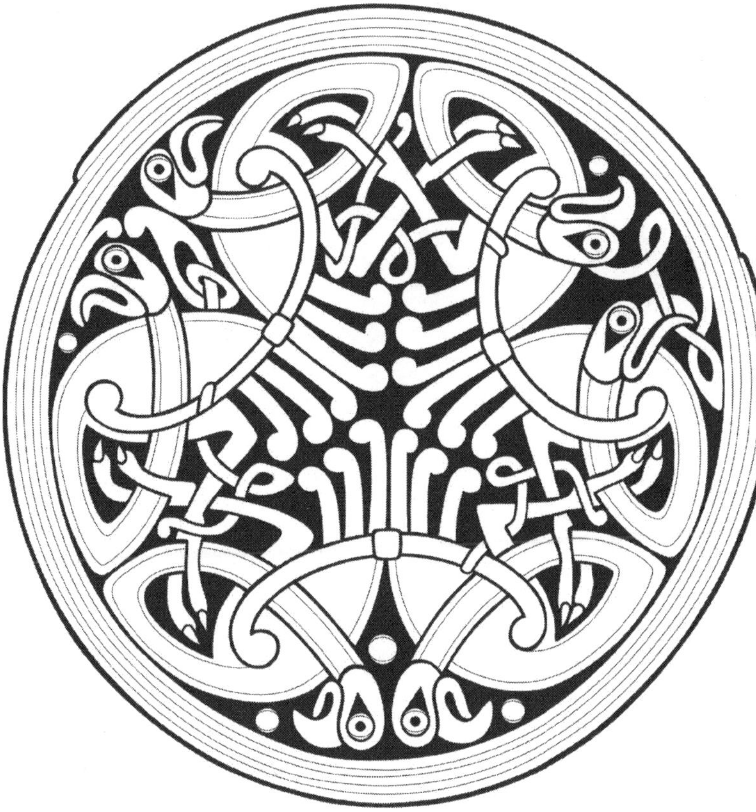

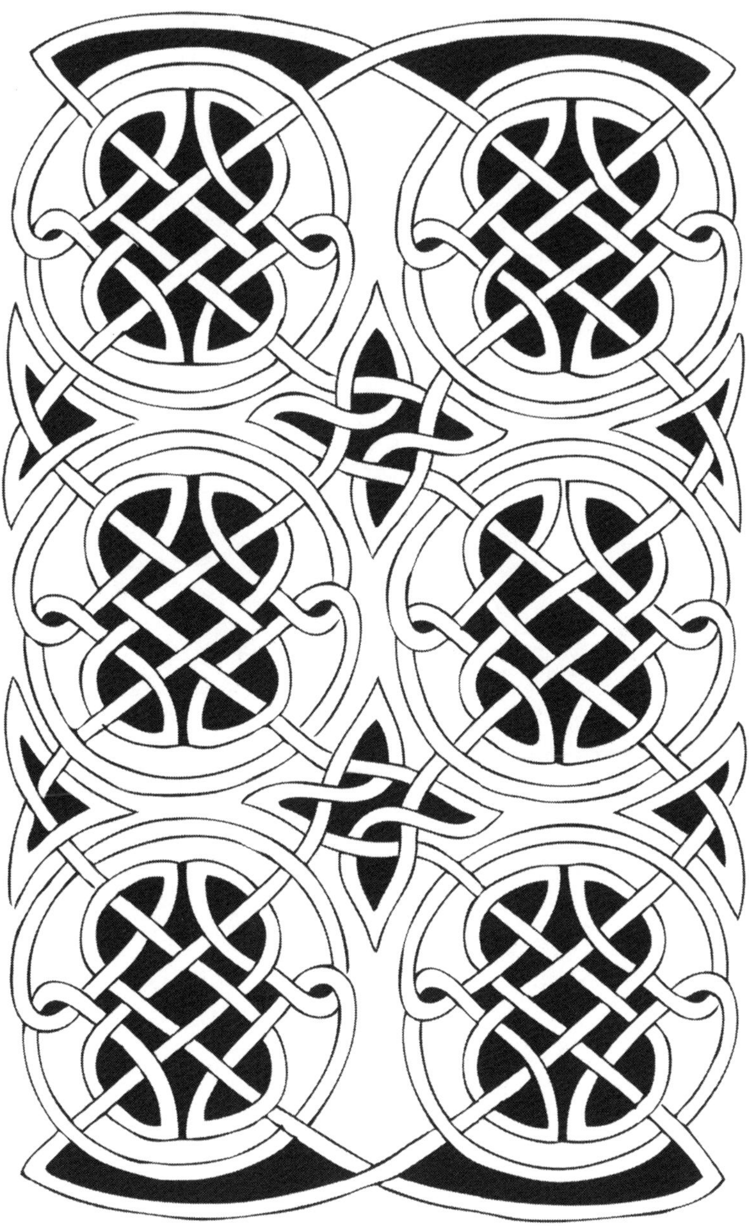

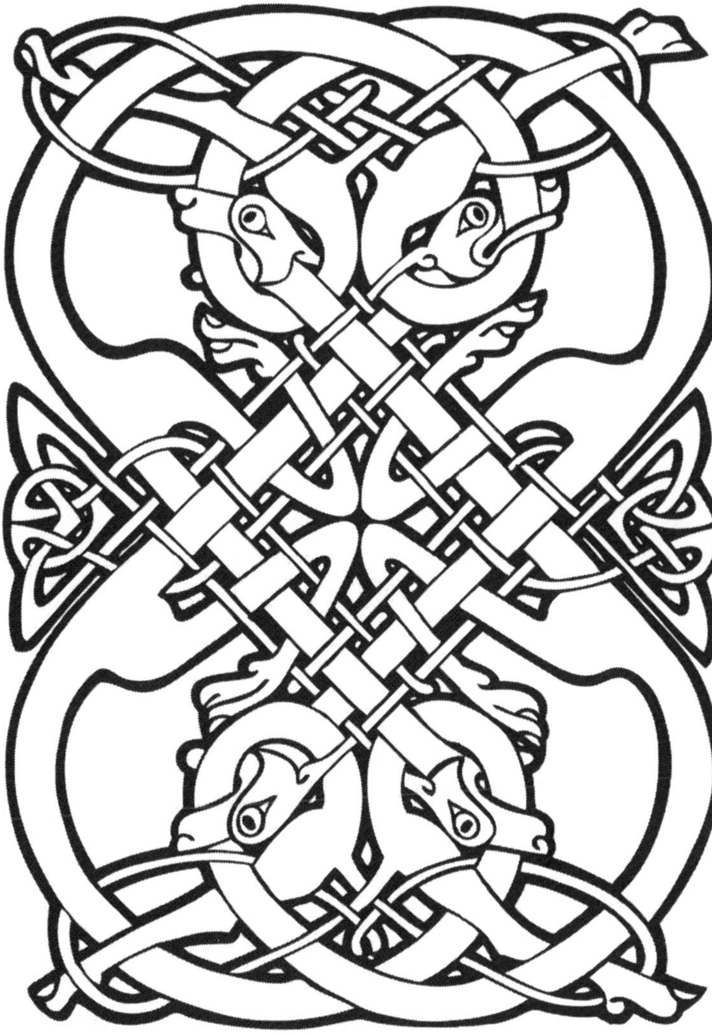

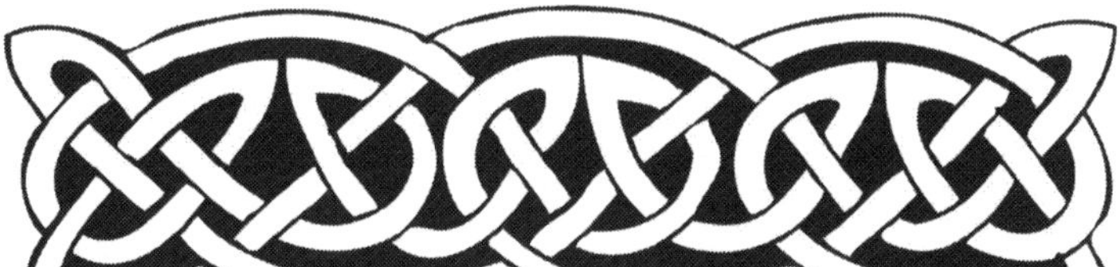

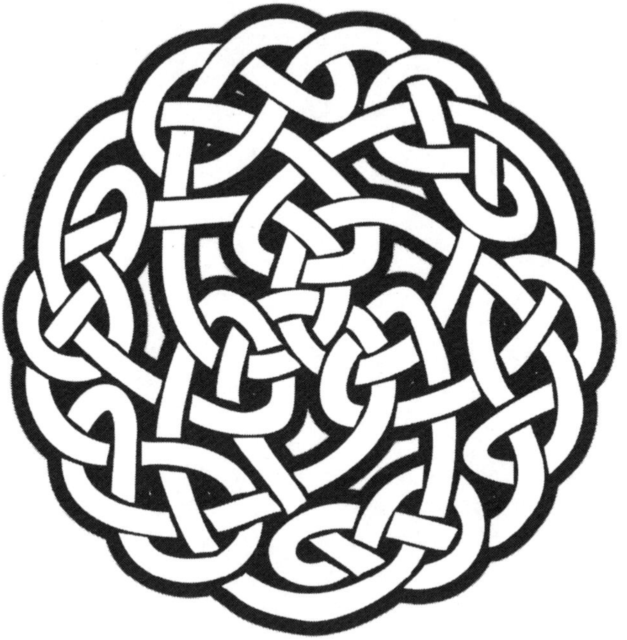

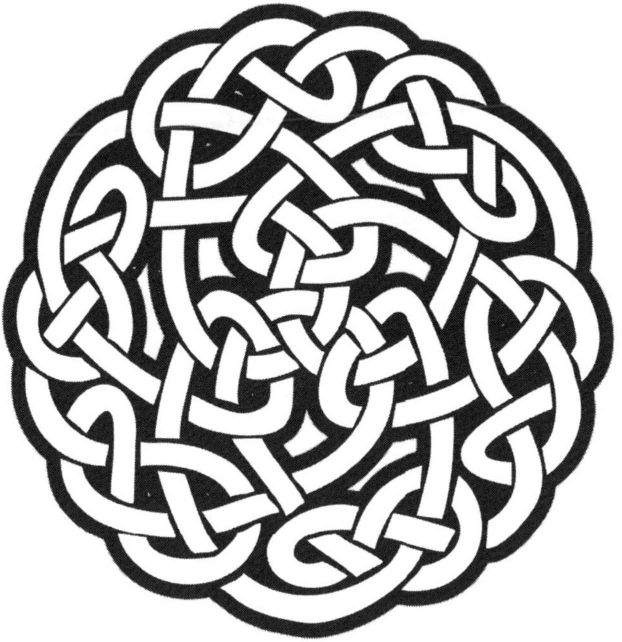

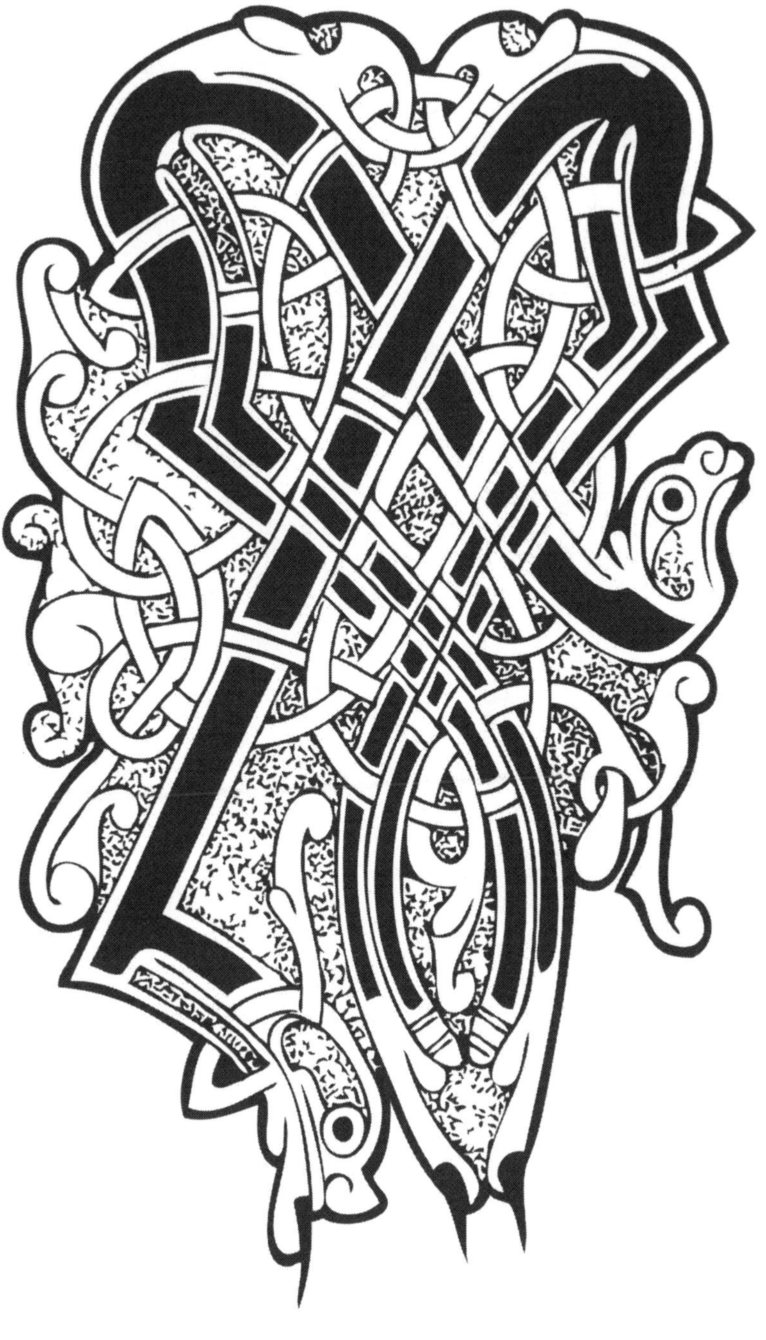

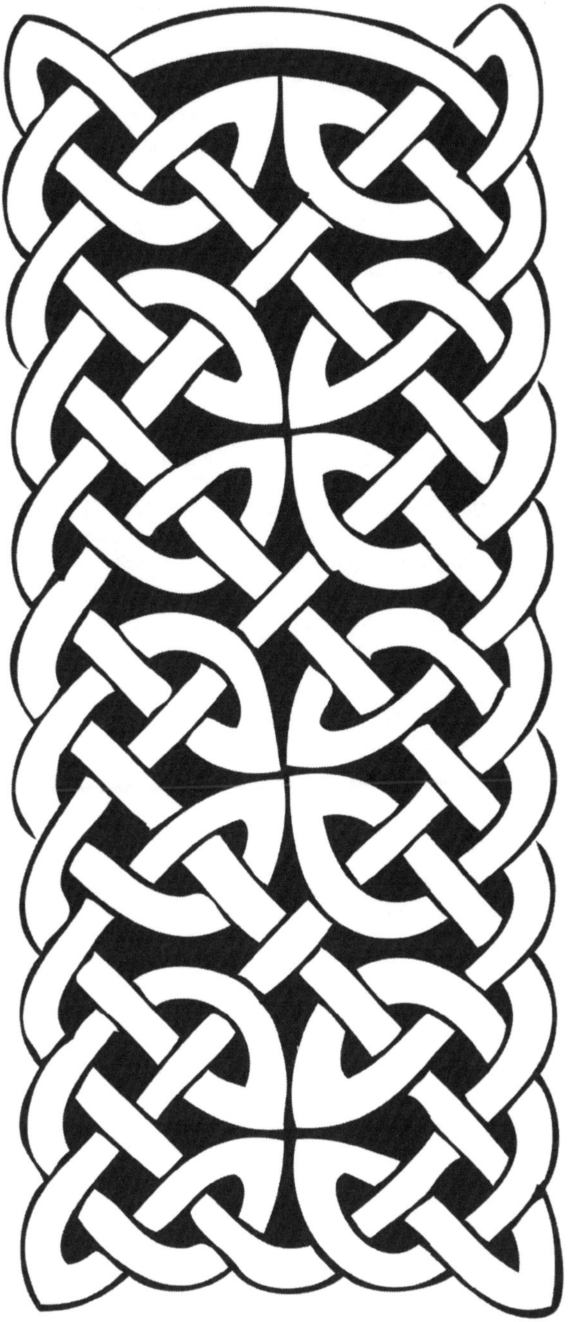

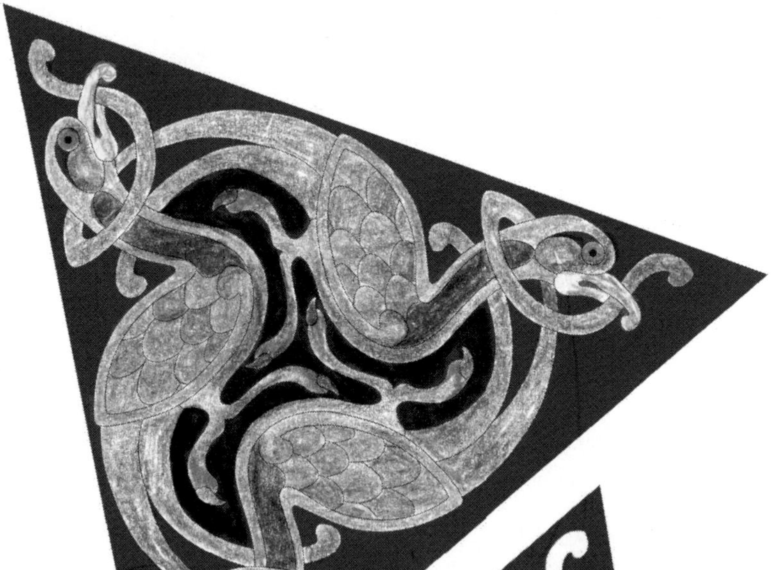

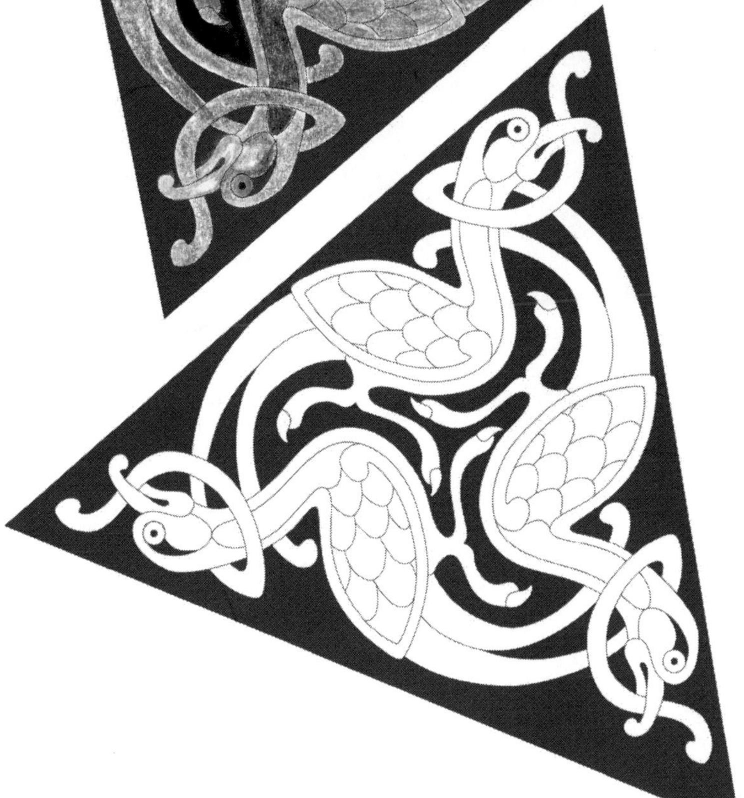

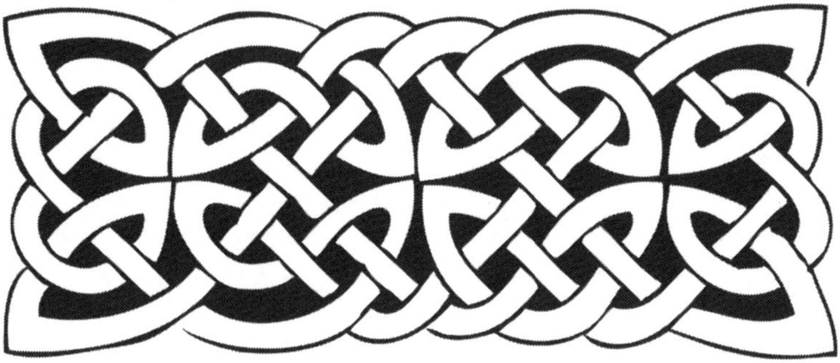

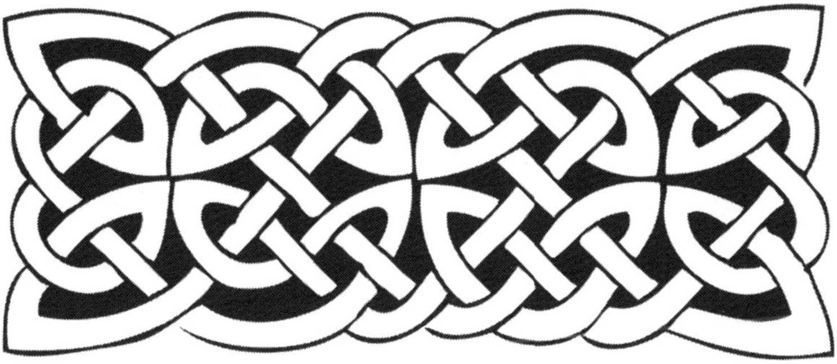

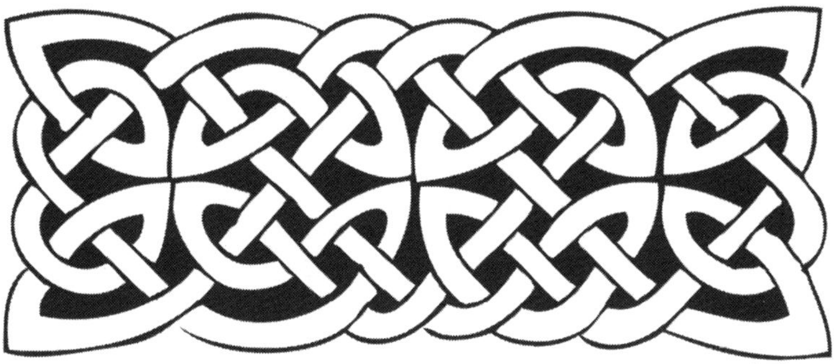

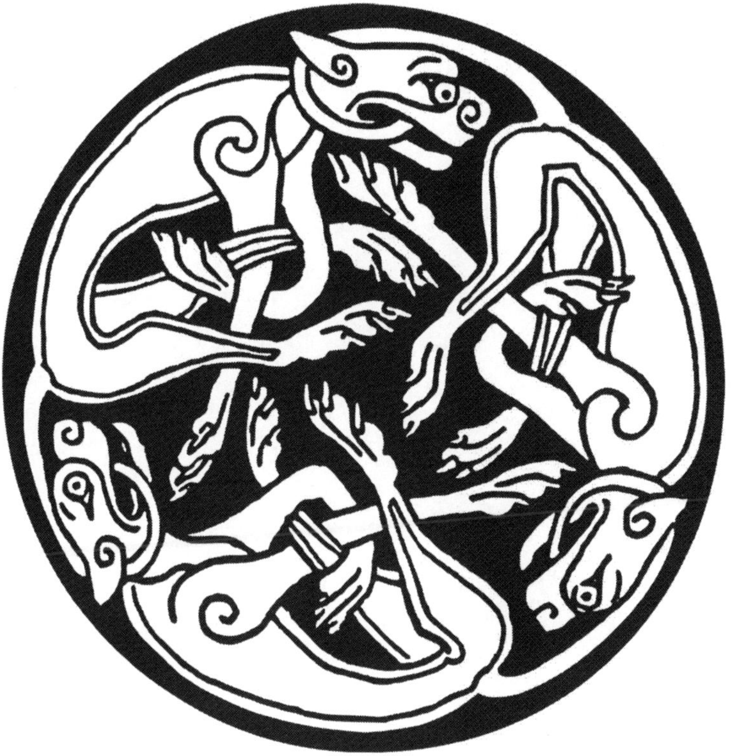

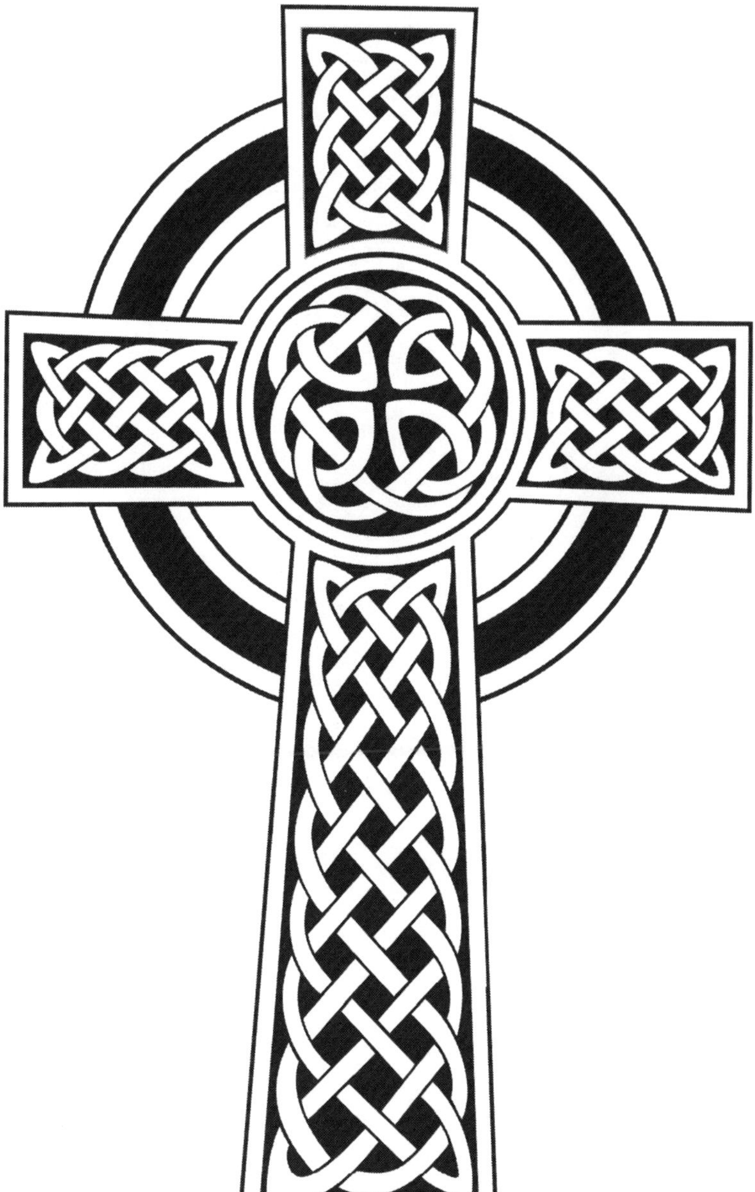

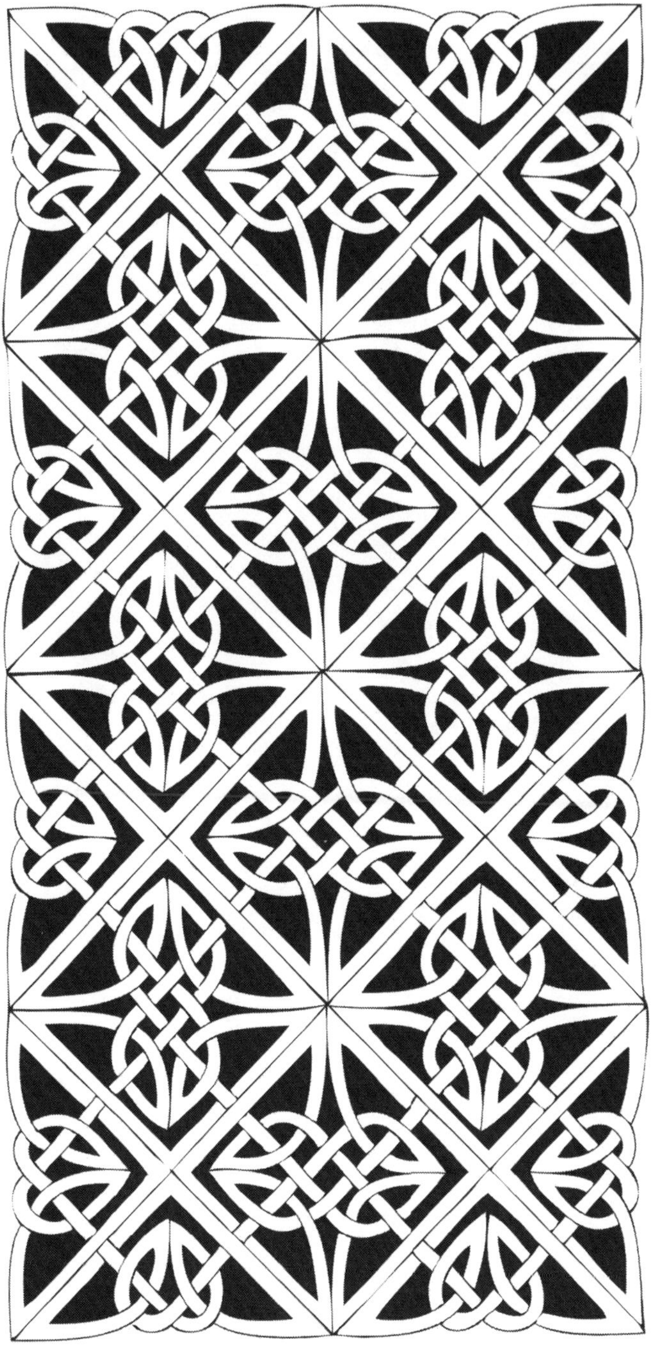

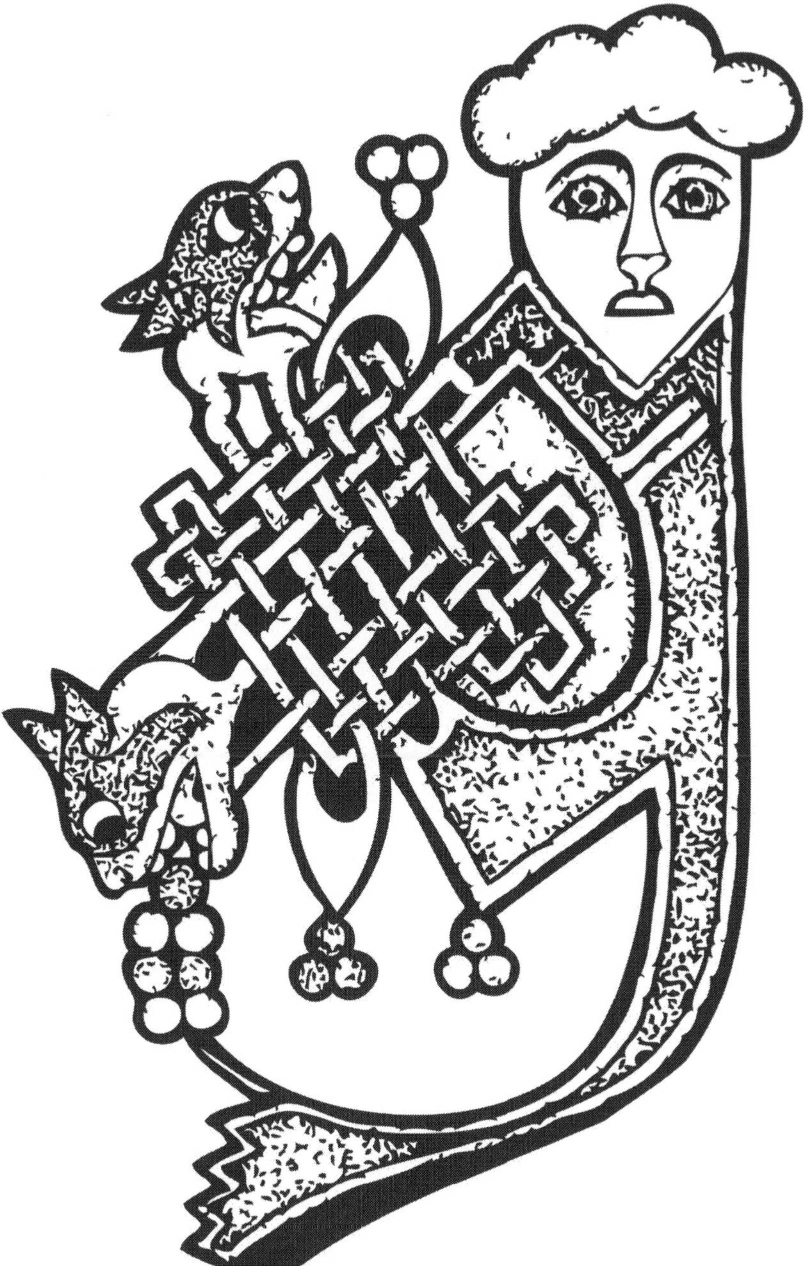

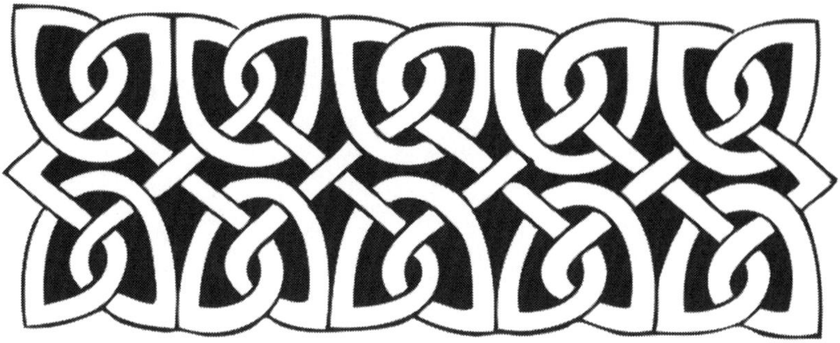

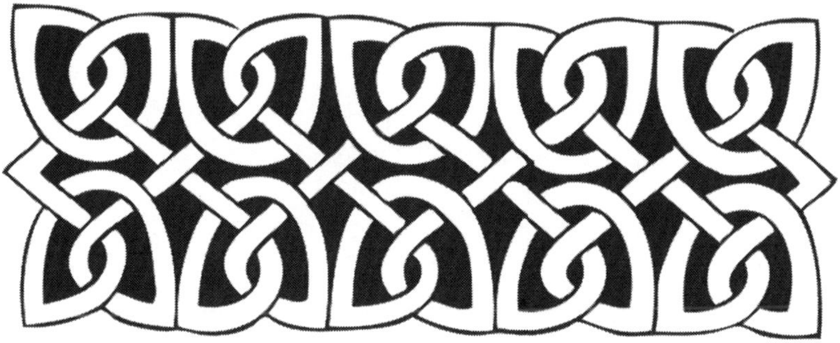

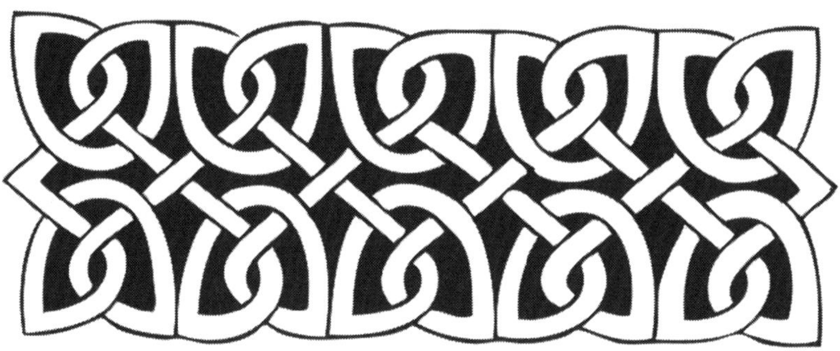

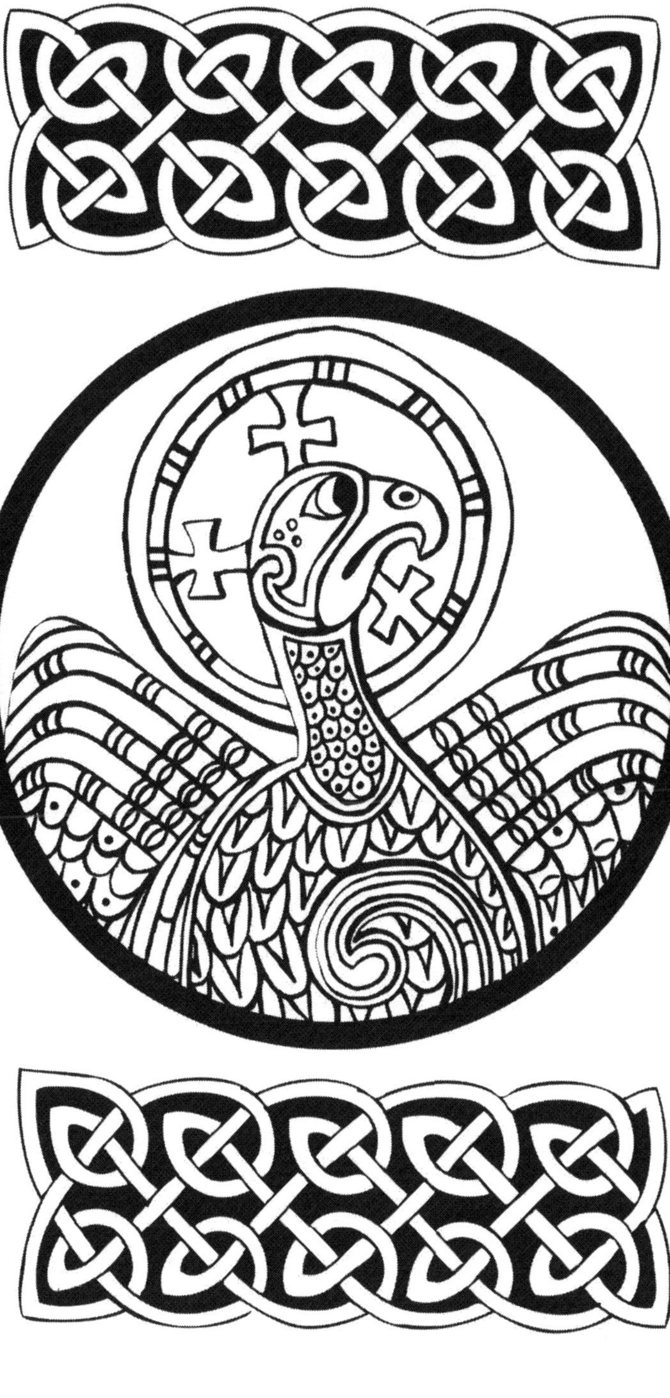

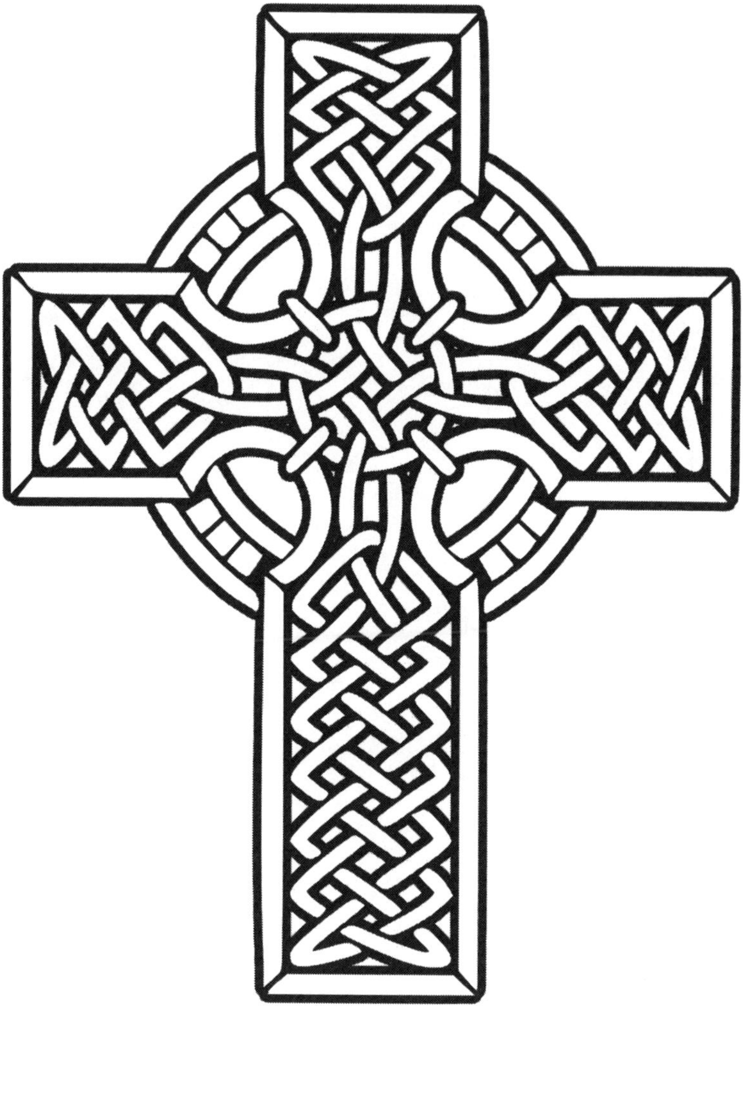

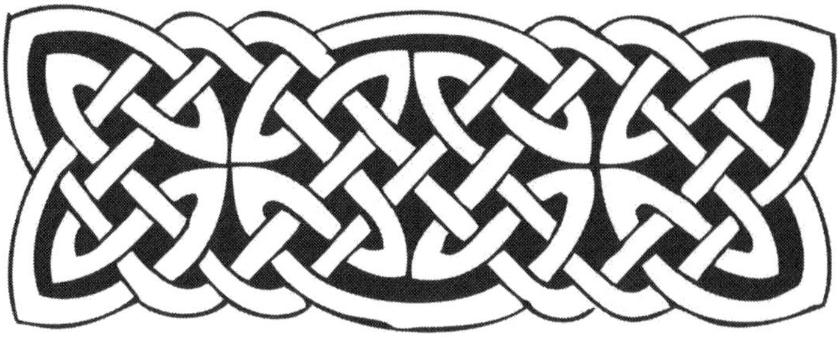
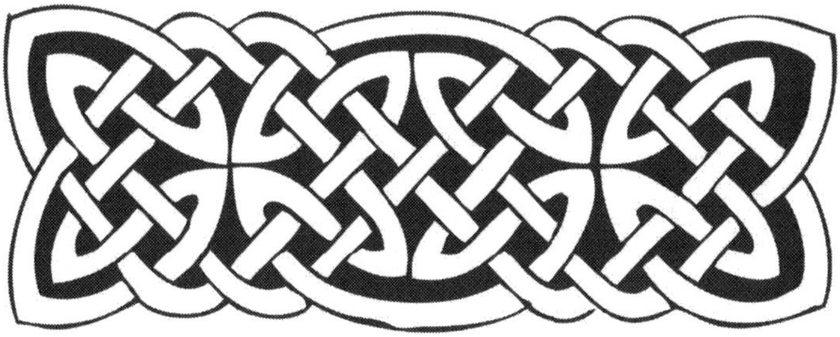
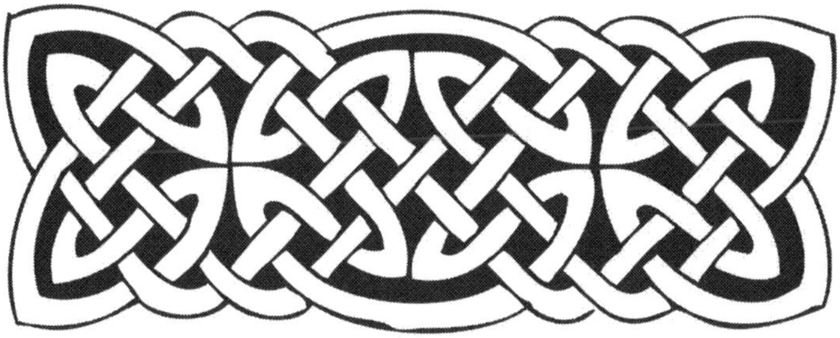
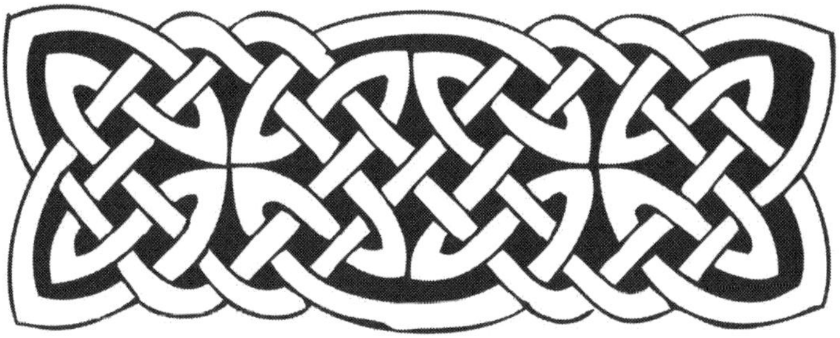

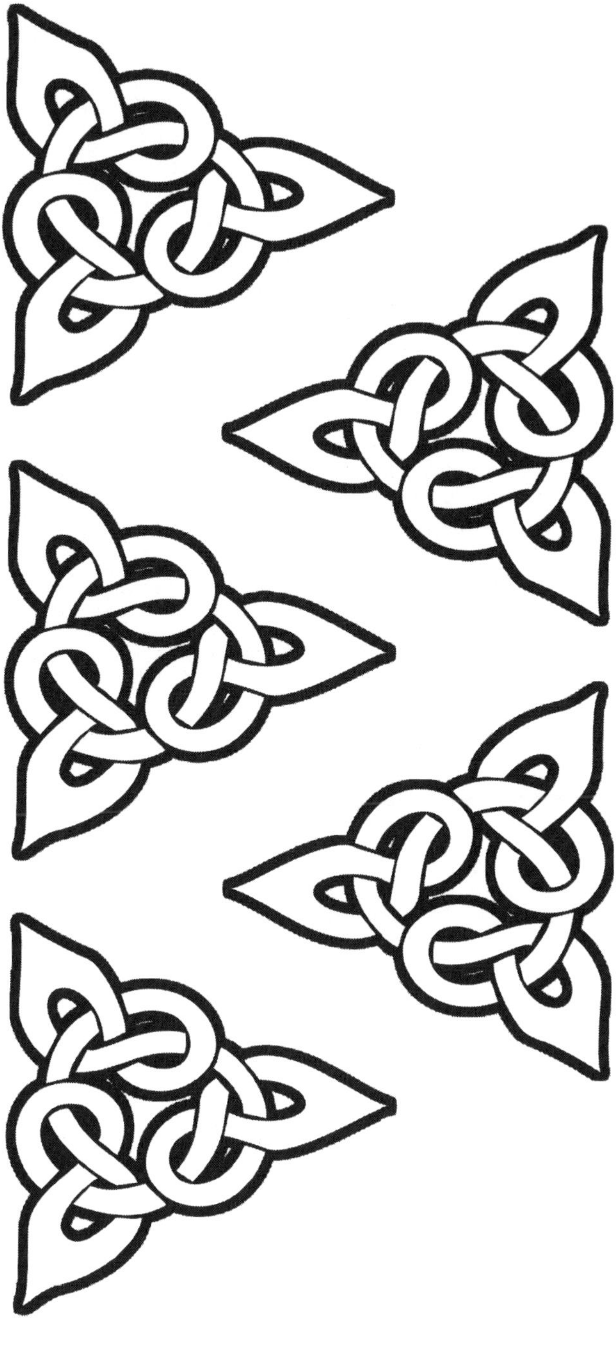

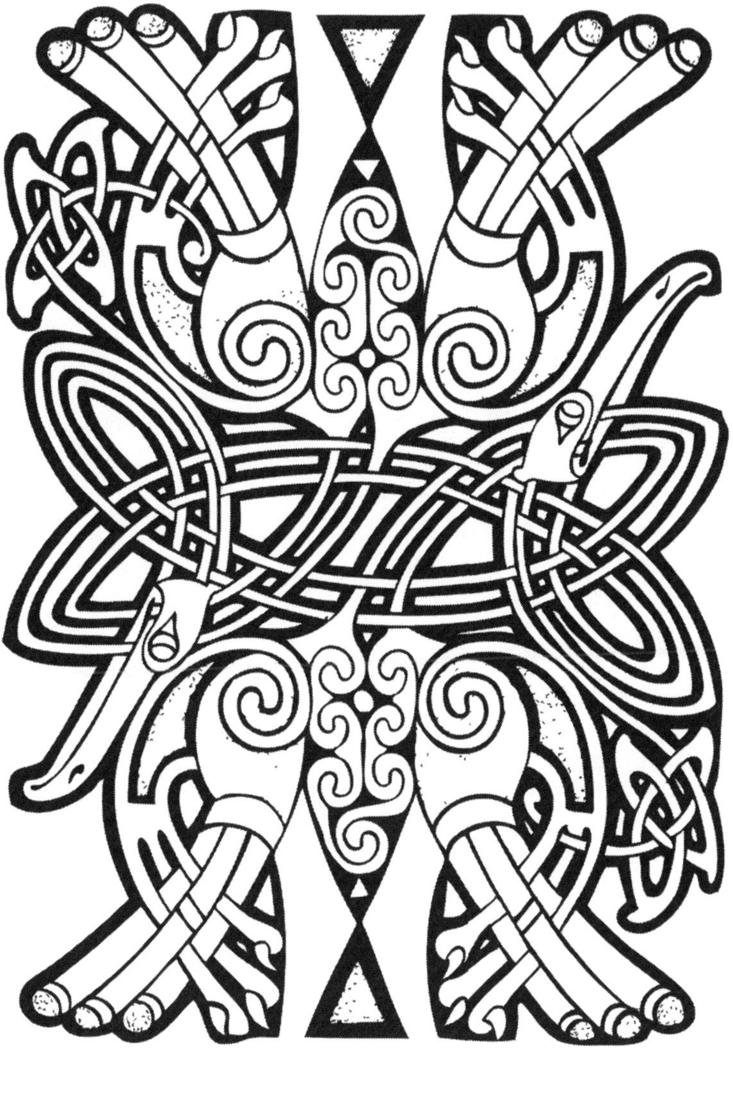

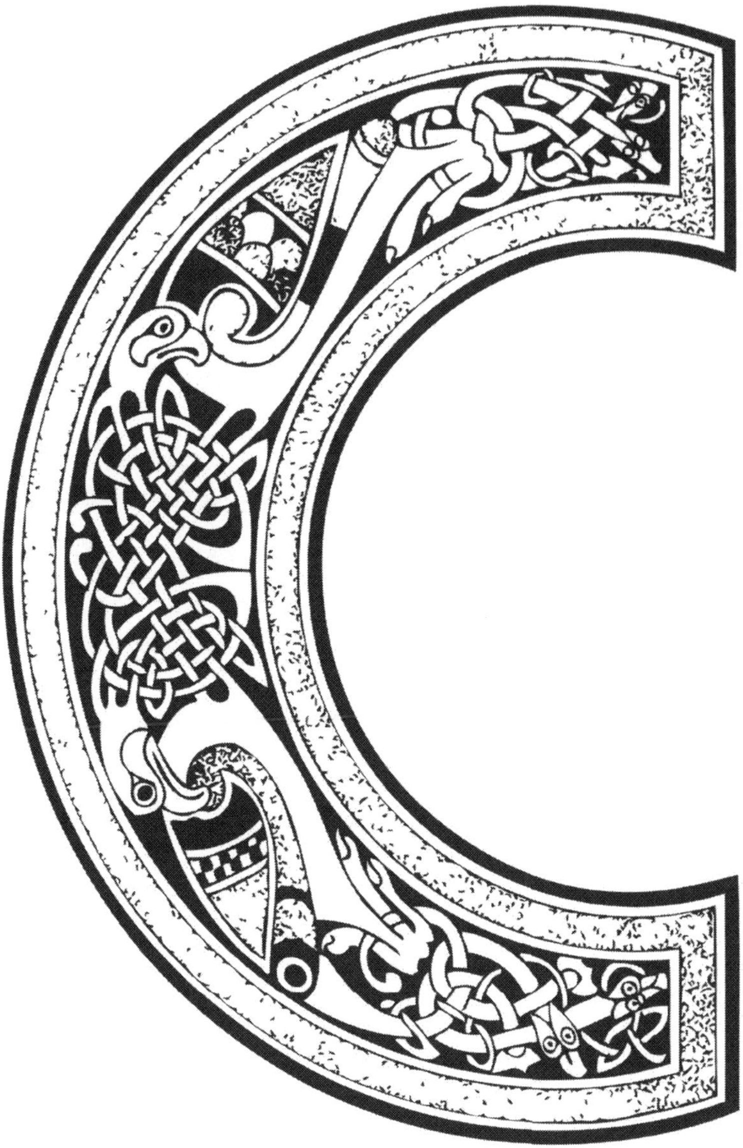

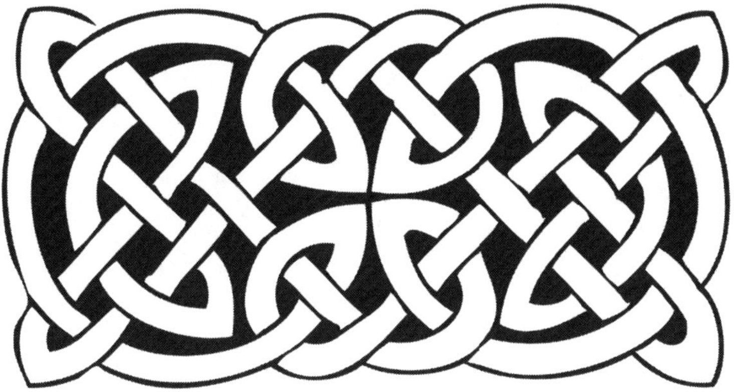

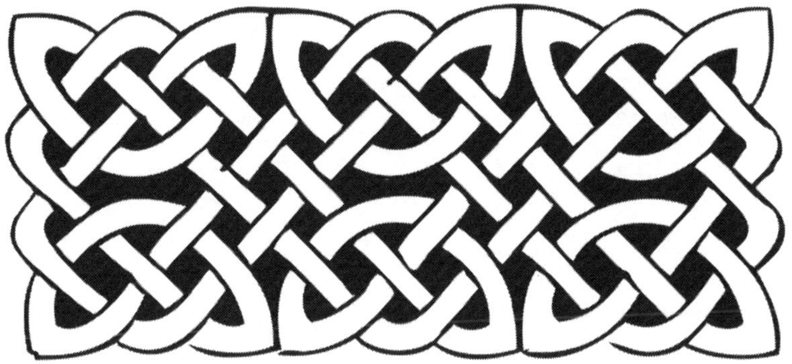

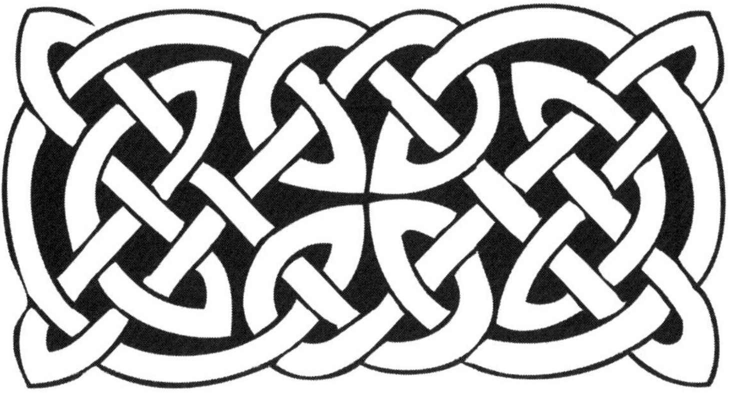

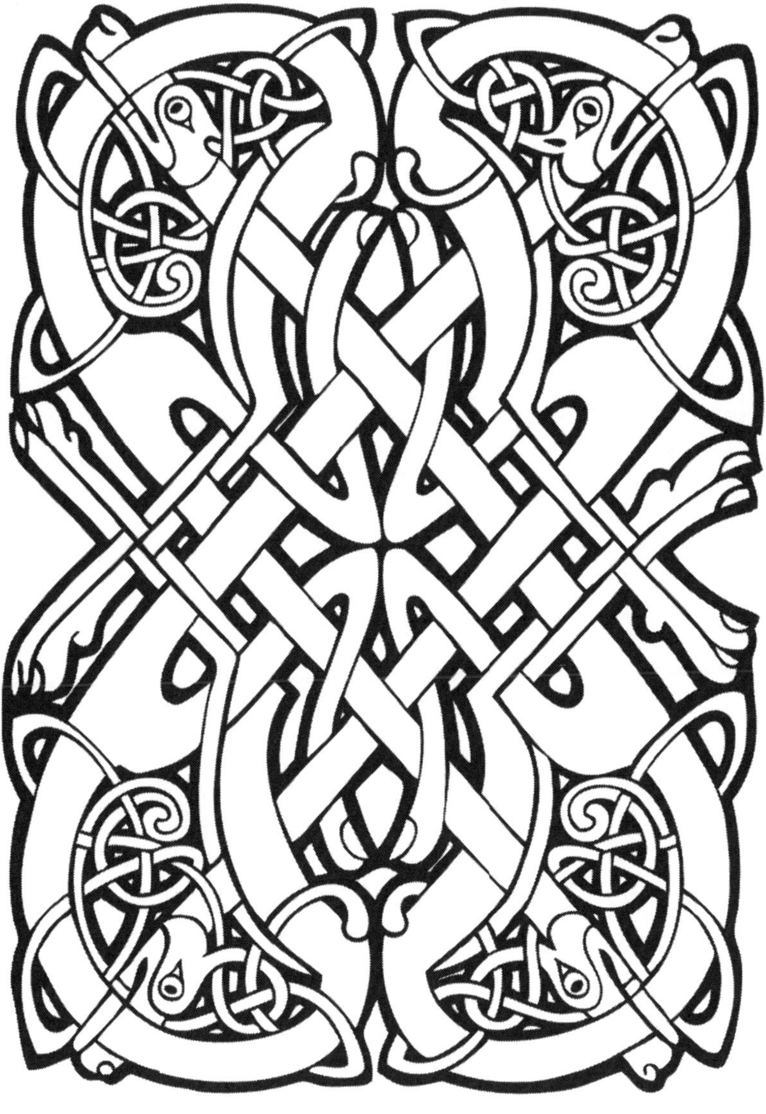

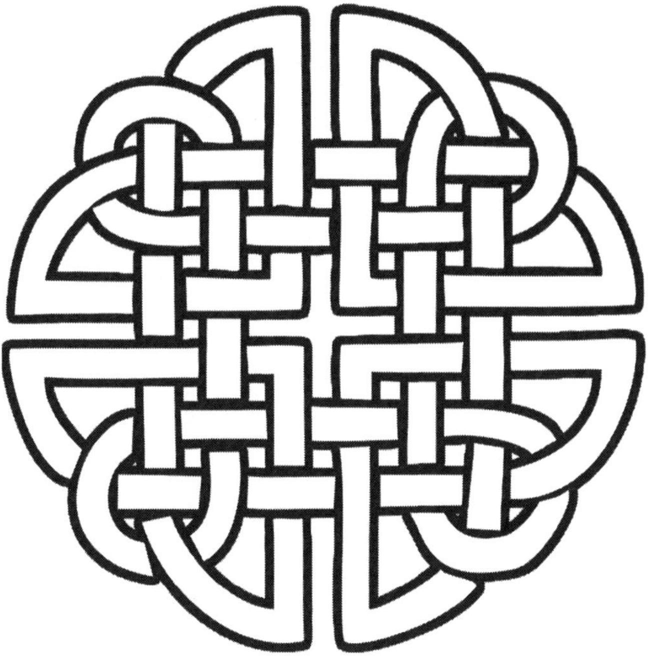

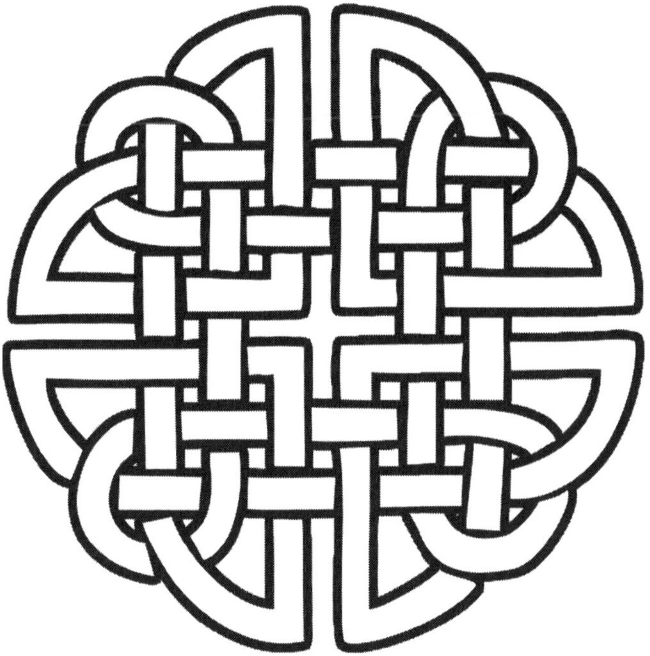

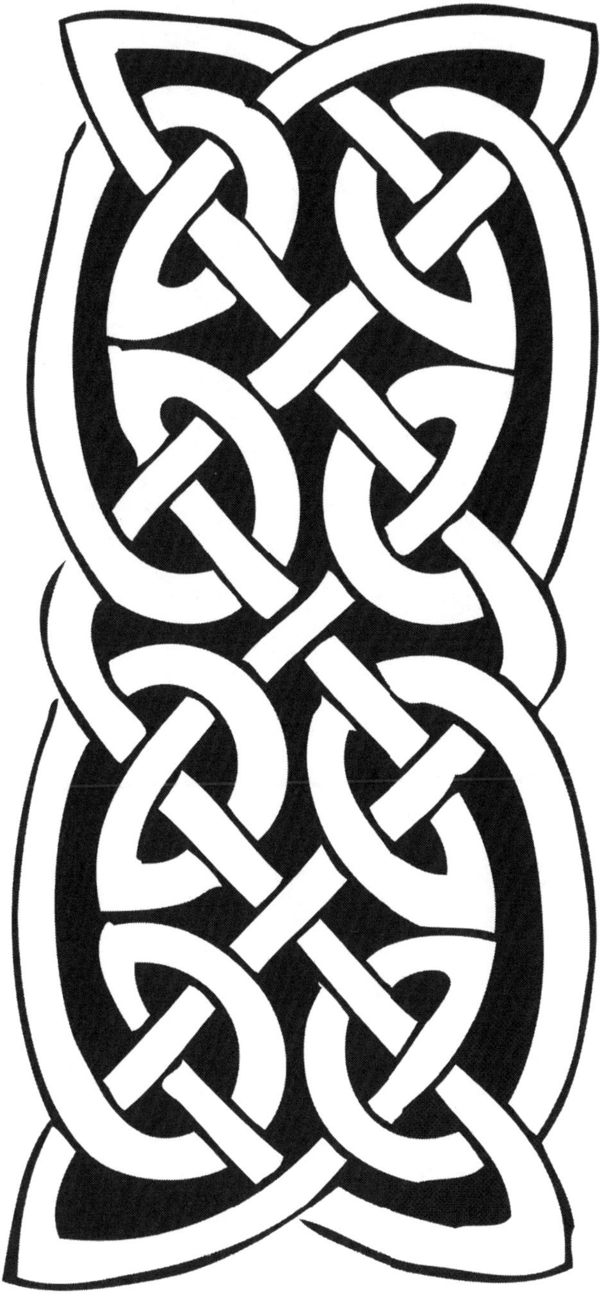

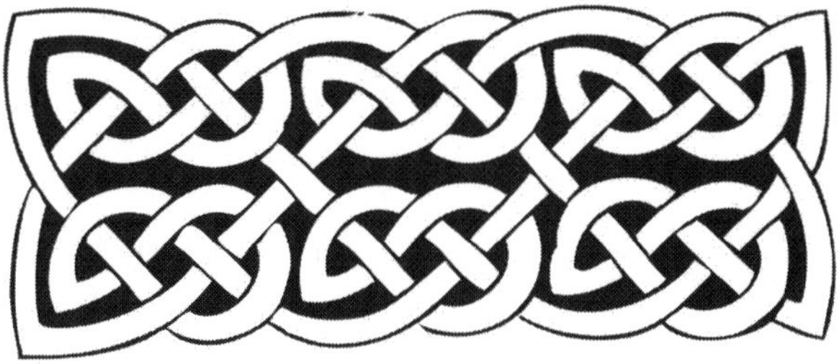

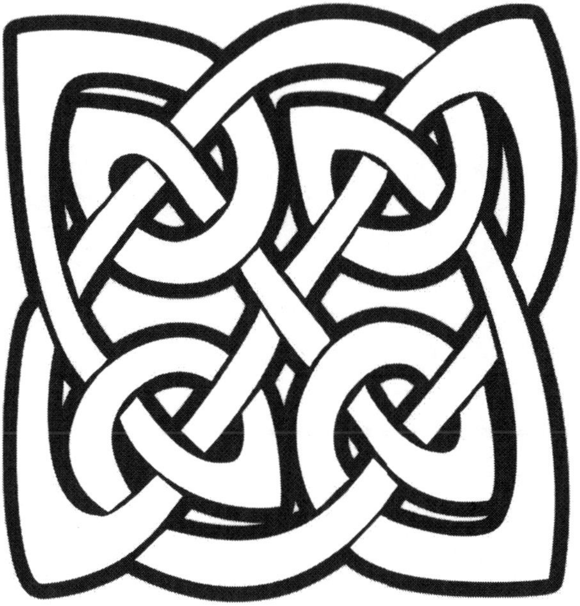

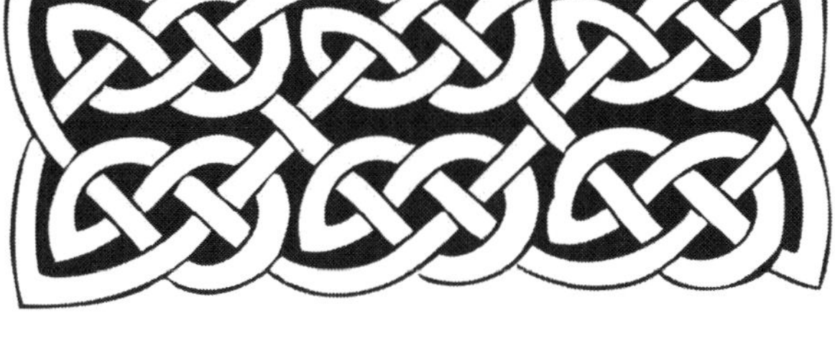

Made in the USA
Columbia, SC
04 March 2021

33913707R00031